Bringing up baby

The illustrated guide to raising humans

Edited by Pam Sommers

CHRONICLE BOOKS

SAN FRANCISCO

Dedication

To Peter
and to
Cathy, Jana,
and Sharon

Acknowledgments

Thanks to all the artists who found time between
deadlines to devote their talents to this collection . . . especially
those who have kids to deal with at the same time!

Thanks to Bill LeBlond, Leslie Jonath, and everyone at Chronicle Books
who liked this new project and agreed to let me loose again.

Special thanks to Sarah Putman for
helping me avoid grammatical embarrassment.

Library of Congress Cataloging-in-Publication Data:
Bringing up baby: the illustrated guide to raising humans / edited by Pam sommers.
p. cm
ISBN 0-8118-0886-6
1. Child rearing—Caricatures and cartoons. 2. American wit and humor, Pictorial.
I. Sommers, Pam
NC1427.B75 1996
741.5'—dc20
96-6755
CIP
Printed in the United States. Distributed in Canada by Raincoast Books
8680 Cambie Street, Vancouver, B.C. V6P 6M9

10 8 6 4 2 1 3 5 7 9

Book design by Catherine Marick
Cover illustration by Greg Clarke

Chronicle Books
275 Fifth Street
San Francisco, CA 94103

Contents

Introduction

Whether or not we have children of our own, we have all had childhoods and witnessed children being raised by relatives, friends, and neighbors and in movies, TV shows, books, and public places.

A process once guided by varying degrees of common sense, intuition, and family custom, child rearing became codified only in the last century or so. From early ladies' magazines, patent medicine broadsides, and etiquette books to Dr. Spock and the current crop of publications doling out "infallible" advice, the subject has been addressed from every possible angle, in dozens of conflicting opinions, serving mostly to confuse and terrify the modern parent.

From the instant they hand you the kid to the day it leaves the nest, your life is filled with decisions both monumental and minute. Do it mostly right and you contribute a good citizen to the planet. Mess up and we might be talking Jeffrey Dahmer or Newt Gingrich.

Since artists are by nature observant and imaginative souls, they seemed to me an excellent group to tap for child-rearing insights. Having directed the Illustration Gallery for six years and collaborated with eighty-four illustrators on an earlier book, I knew just how to start.

I called artists who I thought would have something edifying to say on the subject, and told them each that, hands-on experience or not, this was their opportunity to make a contribution towards molding the next generation. I asked for dos, don'ts, hints, tips, warnings, family customs and traditions, or perhaps a fond (or appalling) memory from their own childhoods.

What I received was a witty and thoughtful, though sometimes pessimistic, mix of perspectives, reflecting the diversity of the contributors themselves.

Eric Hanson tells of his delight in defining childhood landmarks in map drawings, a pleasure now shared with his own son. In appropriate retro style, Daniel Kirk shares a 1950s memory of the havoc caused when his mother thought him lost in a department store and, with no words at all, Christopher Brown depicts his childhood in a puzzle of intriguing symbols.

Taking a cynical view, Joost Swarte draws parents harnessed and ridden by a crowned "prince." Anita Kunz's grown-ups are marionettes in the hand of a giant infant and bleakest of all are Douglas Fraser's yoked, blindered, seemingly lobotomized adults, drawn onward by baby toys dangling from sticks.

Acknowledging the fatigue factor of the superhuman demands of child rearing, William Joyce's looming, drooling "Jackzilla," appeasable only by mother's milk, is simply hilarious, as are Greg Clarke's nine-minute Jekyll and Hyde–like slice of a tot's life and Makiko Azakami's charming but exhausting "Day With Rei."

For pure sweetness, Charles Barsotti and his grandson collaborate on their views of spring and J. Otto Seibold builds a no-frills playhouse for his girls, made magical by his unmistakable shared delight in its creation. Paul Meisel provides sensible advice on safely entering a baby's room in the dark and Tim Lewis offers the gentlest, most practical way of dealing with a child's temporary tic.

As a childless "civilian" I may have a dubious right to add to the canon of child-rearing literature. Looking around me, though, it seems as if parents, like anyone else, could use an extra laugh or two and I thought a *picture* book of advice might be just what was missing from child-rearing bookshelves across the land.

I hope you enjoy the following advice on the art of "bringing up baby" with minimum misery, maximum joy!

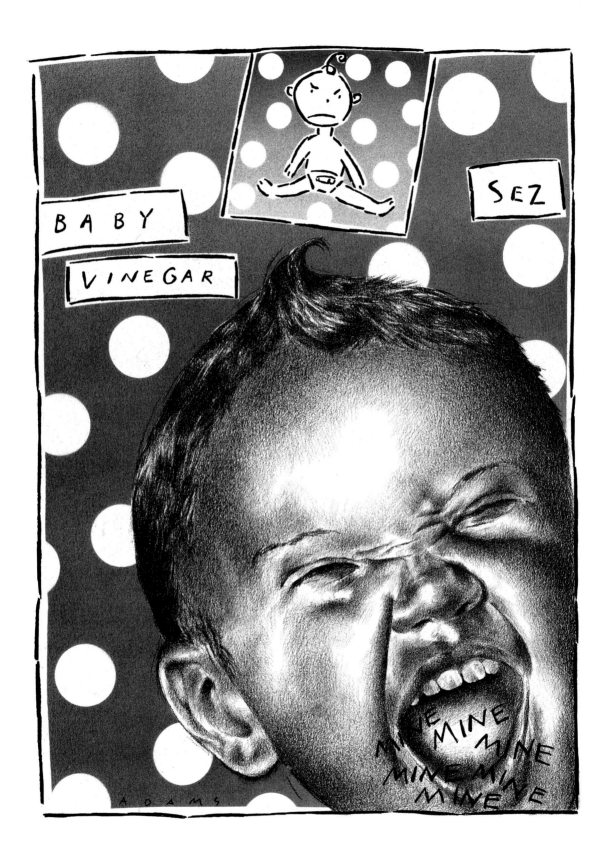

Lisa Adams

Maciek Albrecht

Makiko Azakami

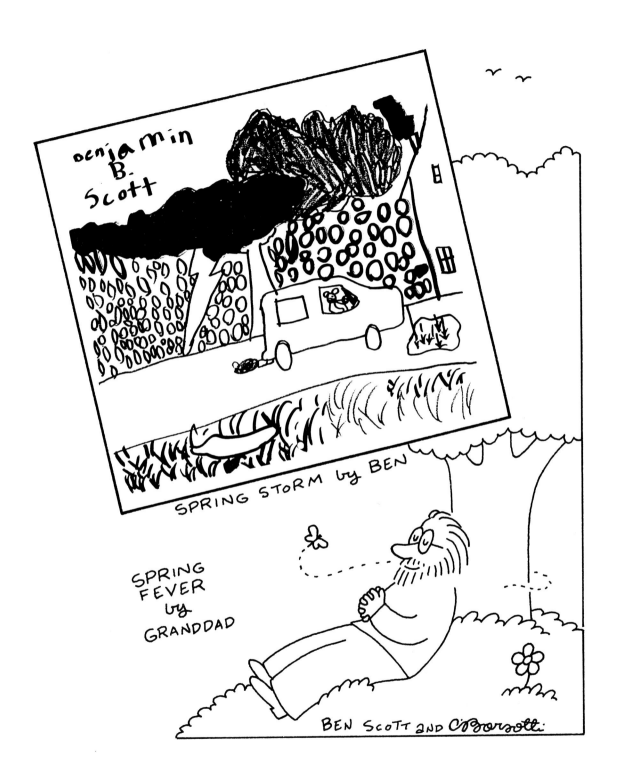

Charles Barsotti

How Do Kool Kids Make the Scene?

Scary Mary

Pumpkin Head Fred

Lizard Liz

Empire State Bill

Hairy Barry

Boney Tony

Marsha Martian

© '95 M.B.

They Trick or Treat on Halloween!

Gary Baseman

WHEN I WAS A BOY I WAS FASCINATED WITH THE GRAND ORGAN STANDING IN THE CATHEDRAL. I WAS CONVINCED THAT MANY ROWS OF PIPES STOOD BEHIND THOSE MAGNIFICENTLY ALIGNED IN THE FRONT.
IT TURNED OUT THAT THERE WERE NONE ...
THIS WAS A MAJOR DISAPPOINTMENT: SUDDENLY THE GREAT INSTRUMENT APPEARED HOLLOW, LIKE A THEATRE SET. INDEED, SOME OF THE PIPES DID NOT WORK, THEY WERE THERE FOR DECORATION ONLY!

Maris Bishofs

Mary Lynn Blasutta

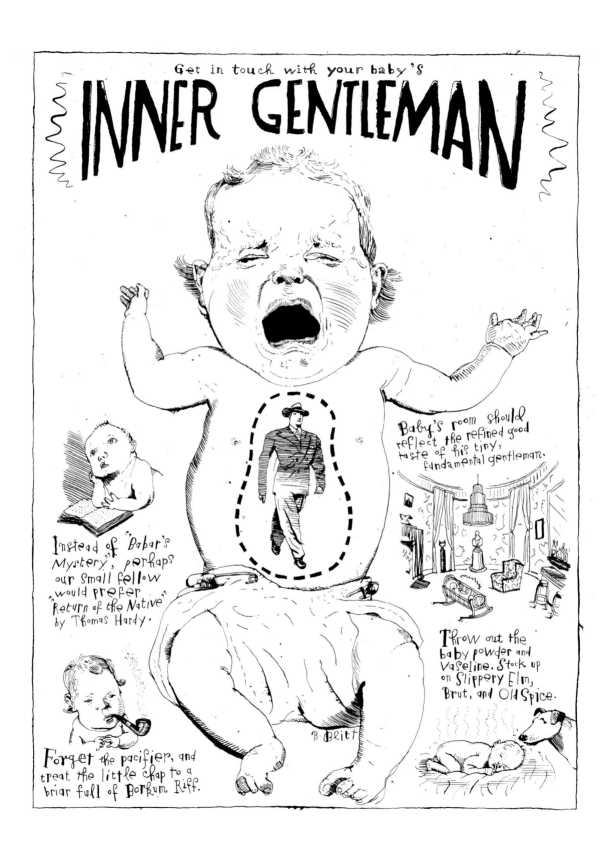

Get in touch with your baby's

INNER GENTLEMAN

Instead of "Babar's Mystery", perhaps our small fellow would prefer "Return of the Native" by Thomas Hardy.

Baby's room should reflect the refined good taste of his tiny, fundamental gentleman.

Throw out the baby powder and Vaseline. Stock up on Slippery Elm, Brut, and Old Spice.

Forget the pacifier, and treat the little chap to a briar full of Borkum Riff.

B. Blitt

Tom Bloom

Christopher S. Brown

Diana Bryan

Dave Calver

VOCATIONAL PRE-SCHOOLS

Roz Chast

HOW TO RAISE A CHILD.

← DRESS WARMLY IN WINTER

IF CRYING SOMETHING MAY BE WRONG.

KEEP AWAY FROM DANGEROUS THINGS.

CHANGE IF WET.

GIVE AN ENEMA ONCE IN A WHILE.

S. CHWAST

WHEN OLD ENOUGH SEND OFF TO COLLEGE.

9 minutes in the Life of Lil' Jack Stoll

4:16pm 4:17pm 4:18pm
4:19pm 4:20pm 4:21pm
4:22pm 4:23pm 4:24pm

Greg Clarke

Paul Corio

Isabelle Dervaux

ONE TIME MY 3 YEAR OLD DAUGHTER JILLIAN COULD NOT GO WITH HER MOTHER TO TAE KWON DO AND SHE THREW A FIT—RUNNING AROUND THE HOUSE SPITTING AT ME AND YELLING—SHE HAD EATEN CANDY ALL DAY LONG AT HER EASTER PARTY AT PRESCHOOL

Go Out To The GaRAGE!

March 1965   R. Egielski

Sister Generosa wanted
to know why I didn't sell
more chances. I said, "because
I stayed home to watch The
Rolling Stones on The Clay
Cole Show."

El Niño

c. fisher

Carolyn Fisher

Jeffrey Fisher

Douglas Fraser

Constantly Encourage Self-Expression

gale

Janie Geiser

David Goldin

DISPENSE AS NEEDED

One hug for the following symptoms:

1) bruised knee
2) hurt feelings
3) lost puppy
4) broken toy
5) wounded heart

Symptoms may vary.

Julia Gorton

KIDS!

They think they're REALLY clever

They think LIFE is a bowl of Cherries

They think MONEY grows on trees

PARENTS! don't be fooled

Josh Gosfield

If your kids don't eat this
- *they're just not hungry.*

Bob found it easier to mold clay.

Gene Greif

Up to a certain age, if you draw something, it becomes real. After that point, forget it.

Steven Guarnaccia

When I was a KID 😀, I
drew MAPS of everything.
My room, our YARD, the
neighborhood, especially of
the 🌳 WOODS near our 🏠
house. Drawn in were landmarks
like Hollow Trees, hiding places,
friend's houses, other STUFF.

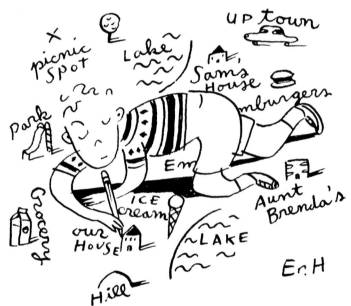

NOW I ✏️ draw maps
with MY Son 😄. His favorites
are Treasure Maps. 🎁 If
you can draw maps you will
always know where you have
been.

Eric Hanson

Jessie Hartland

Pamela Hobbs

⇒ CHILDREN · ARE · OVERBEARING
SUPERCILIOUS · PASSIONATE ·
ENVIOUS · INQUISITIVE · IDLE
FICKLE
TIMID · INTEMPERATE
LIARS
AND · DISSEMBLERS
THEY · LAUGH
AND · WEEP
EASILY · ARE
EXCESSIVE
IN · THEIR · JOYS · AND
SORROWS.
AND · THAT · ABOUT
THE · MOST
TRIFLING
OBJECTS · THEY
BEAR · NO · PAIN
BUT · LIKE · TO
INFLICT · IT · ON
· OTHERS ·

ALREADY · THEY · ARE · MEN.

David Johnson

You can try the most amazing

hairdos on kids and they will

let you. They know how to have fun. Maira Kalman

SOME fun things TO Do

By Vikki Kann

Look Ma, We're a siamese twin!

Play Dress -u

Make a drink that Takes you back in time.

🦴 + Wesson Oil 🦋 + QUICK QUAKER OATS =

First Imagine the TIME period you waNt to go Back to. Then Add lots of different ingredients. (Have your beSt fRiend DRiNk it to See if it works)

WatCH MicKEy

WRiTE Your MemoirS

Dear Diary,   Date April
Thursday
Today in school Harvey made a funny face by crossing his eyes and sticking out his big tongue. Then Norman slapped him on his back and Harveys eyes got stuck!!

BE FIRM WITH YOUR CHILDREN.

Bruce Eric Kaplan

"... And Junior Will Have His 'To Go.'"

EVEN IF YOUR TODDLER IS PAST THE STAGE OF WHINING AND DINING, YOU'LL WANT TO TAKE PRECAUTIONS AT YOUR ROMANTIC TABLE FOR TWO-AND-A-HALF.

ALTHOUGH MOST RESTAURANTS WILL GLADLY PROVIDE A HIGH CHAIR OR BOOSTER SEAT, PARENTS WHO WANT TO AVOID A TOSSED SALAD MIGHT CONSIDER BRINGING A CHILDREN'S CAR SEAT (WITH SAFETY BELT AND SHOULDER STRAPS).

AT VERY LEAST, BRING YOUR TODDLER'S OWN BIB, SOME CRAYONS OR SOFT TOYS, AND A GENEROUS GRATUITY.

SEAN KELLY

introducing.......
the minus two quartet + 1*

J.D. King

*raised as jazz music prodigies
this trio makes no apologies
they're here t' blow and swing
'cuz red hot & cool is their thing

Adventure at Penney's, 1954

Little Danny thought it funny, hiding from his mom.
"We'll find your boy," the store detective said, "now, just stay calm!"
But panic gripped the mother's mind; she always feared the worst.
She raced from aisle to aisle, and cried as if her heart would burst.
Could he have been abducted to some vile kidnapper's lair?
Or was he lying, broken, at the bottom of a stair?
Soon all the store employees left their posts, and joined the search.
Prayers for Danny's safe return were offered up in church.
At last, the missing boy was found by one resourceful clerk;
beneath a counter, safe and sound, slept naughty Danny Kirk.

Daniel Kirk

"Don't worry about the Kids —they're just out playing..."

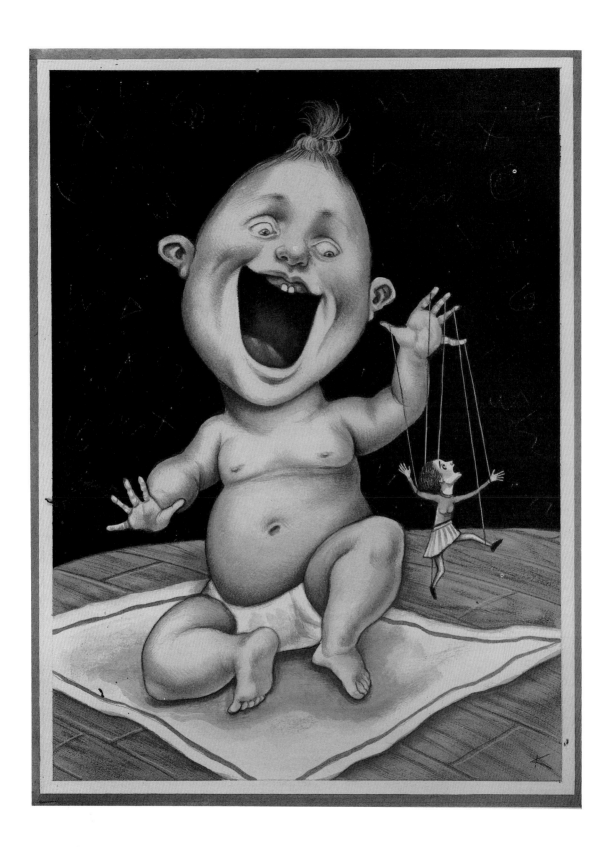

Anita Kunz

A MODEST PROPOSAL

For Preventing the Children of Poor People from Being a Burden to Their Parents or Country, and for Making Them Beneficial to the Public.

It is a melancholy object to those who walk through this great town when they see the streets crowded with beggars.

Homeless Please help

Having turned my thoughts upon this important subject,

I fortunately fell upon this proposal, which is wholly new, and of no expense. I shall now therefore humbly propose my own thoughts, which I hope will not be liable to the least objection.

I have been assured by a very knowing American, that a young healthy child well nursed is a most delicious, nourishing, and wholesome food, whether stewed, roasted, baked, or broiled, and I make no doubt that it will equally serve in a fricassee or ragout.

I grant this food will be somewhat dear, and therefore very proper for landlords, who, as they have already devoured most of the parents, seem to have the best title to the children.

Besides having a new dish introduced to the tables of all gentlemen of fortune, the money will circulate among ourselves, the goods being entirely of our own manufacture.

Many other advantages might be enumerated. For instance, the constant breeders gain by the sale of their children. This would be a great inducement to marriage. And it would increase the care and tenderness of mothers toward their children.

Men would become as fond of their wives during the pregnancy as they now are of their cows in calf, their sows when they are ready to farrow.

I desire those who dislike my overture to attempt to answer the impossibility of paying rent without money or trade.

I profess I have not the least interest in endeavoring to promote this necessary work. But I have no other motive than the public good of my country, by providing for infants, relieving the poor, and giving some pleasure to the rich.

Essay by Jonathan Swift (1667—1745)
Illustrations by Peter Kuper (1958—   )

Philippe Lardy

Once upon a time ... a very young daughter of mine developed a habit of opening and closing her mouth widely and quickly, kind of like a lickety-split yawn.

Time passed but not the yawn.

Finally, I asked her why she did this and she replied, "To let the la-las out."

Fearing that any further discussion of la-las might risk the possibility of her carrying them into spinsterhood, I said nothing.

Either they just went away or she expelled them all.

A disappearing la-la.

Leave la-las alone and they'll move on.

STAN MACK'S REAL LIFE FUNNIES: MAN TO MAN
ALL DIALOGUE GUARANTEED VERBATIM

"THANK YOU ALL VERY MUCH. I'D JUST LIKE TO SAY THAT THESE FIRST FIVE YEARS HAVE BEEN FUN-FILLED YEARS, CHOCK-FULL OF SUNSHINE AND SMILES. TRUE, ALONG WITH THE LAUGHTER WERE SOME TEARS, SOME SETBACKS, SOME BITTER DISAPPOINTMENTS, BUT I HAVE BEEN GIVEN TO BELIEVE THAT SUCH IS LIFE."

Michael Maslin

STRCHRARAYNHH
TYOAAESOMOEBO
AOWTNLEGIJIOO
RUNCDEPRNRGRD

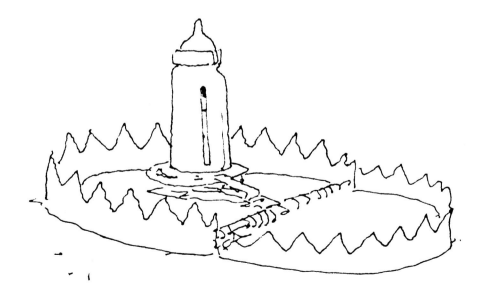

Bill Mayer

JUST SAY...

Patrick McDonnell

When traveling through a child's room at night, it is important to walk
with a shuffling motion, keeping one's feet in constant contact with
the ground while carefully feeling for toys and other hazardous objects.

Paul Meisel

Greg Nemec

Robert Neubecker

BABIES NEED PROTEIN

JUVENILE JUSTICE

MISDEMEANOR

FELONY

CAPITAL CRIME

DON'T FORGET THE SUNBLOCK.

IF YOU CAN'T LOVE AND CARE FOR YOUR KID DON'T MAKE IT.

WILL YOU BE MY DADDY?

YOUR KID IS THE CHILD: YOU ARE THE MATURE ONE.

YELP!

YOU'RE ACTING LIKE A CHILD!

YOUR LIFE WILL NEVER BE THE SAME AGAIN.

ZZZZ

EVER.

HAVING A CHILD IS HAVING A CINEMASCOPE HORROR MOVIE OF POSSIBLE TRAGEDIES IN YOUR MIND AT ALL TIMES, FOREVER

HONK HONK

IF YOU CAN'T SPEND THE TIME IT TAKES TO BE A GOOD PARENT DON'T HAVE A KID.

DON'T HIT YOUR CHILD! TALK TO YOUR KID. THINK!

BABIES ARE LITTLE BABIES FOR JUST A LITTLE WHILE IN GROWN-UP TIME — SAVOUR THE DIFFI-CULTIES. SOON YOU WON'T HAVE THEM. ENJOY THE POOP. POP.

NOTHING MAKES ONE SO VULNER-ABLE AS HAVING RESPON-SIBILITY FOR SOMETHING PRECIOUS BEYOND MEASURE

THAT'S THE WAY IT GOES.

WHEN YOU AREN'T LOOKING YOUR BABY HE WILL KICK OUT OF YOUR ARMS AND HIT THE FLOOR WITH A SICKENING THUD AND BLEED AND YOU WILL FEEL SMALL AND LOW.

BIOLOGY DOESN'T CARE ABOUT YOUR FITNESS TO BE A PARENT

SNORK!

A KID NEEDS A FAMILY. AND LOVE: TO KNOW THAT SHE IS LOVED AND PROTECTED AND FED.

STICK WITH YOUR KID.

IF YOU'RE LUCKY YOU'LL DIE FIRST.

5.23.1995

Evan Polenghi

ONCE, WHEN I WAS NINE YEARS OLD, I SPENT THE NIGHT AT LARRY'S HOUSE.
IT WAS VERY LATE AND EVERYONE WAS IN BED WITH LIGHTS OUT. LARRY AND I WERE
WIDE AWAKE THOUGH; TALKING, HORSING AROUND AND JUST BEING NOISY KIDS.

SUDDENLY, A FIGURE WITH WILDLY SWINGING ARMS CAST A SHADOW
IN THE MOONLIGHT SHINING ON THE BED. THEN, JUST AS SUDDENLY, IT VANISHED.

ALMOST TOO AFRAID TO BREATHE, LET ALONE LOOK OUT THE WINDOW,
WE LAY SOUNDLESS AND FROZEN UNTIL WE FELL ASLEEP.

THE NEXT MORNING WE FOUND OUT THAT LARRY'S DAD, STILL AWAKE
BECAUSE OF OUR RACKET, WAS THE "CRAZY MAN" OUTSIDE THE WINDOW WHO
SCARED US INTO SILENCE AND TO SLEEP!

Kee Rash

How babies get here from where they come from.

Victoria Roberts

There ONce was a
baby named Jacob
who loved to laugh &
hiccup.
He scrambled + crawled +
Liked to 👁 see things
mauled
+ in the end there was
a lot to Pickup.

my
Son   Rogers

Important tip: Think carefully before you speak

J. Otto Seibold

Spare the Rod McKuen and Spoil the Child

Danny Shanahan

Maddalena Sisto

The MAKING of MOSES

HAROLD KRAMER WAS STANDING IN THE OUTFIELD AS I HEADED ACROSS THE SCHOOL PLAYGROUND ON MY WAY TO THE CANDY STORE. HAROLD GLARED AT ME AS I PASSED BY AND I IMPULSIVELY TRIED OUT MY DAD'S HILARIOUS SAYING: "DON'T ROLL YOUR BLOODSHOT EYES AT ME?"

WHOOP WHOOP WHOOP??

ELWOOD H. SMITH ~ ABOUT 1950 ~

Art Spiegelman

Joost Swarte

THE BABY REMOTE

← DON'T PUT THAT IN YOUR MOUTH

← DON'T TOUCH THAT

← DON'T POOP

← POOP

DON'T SPIT UP ON MY SHOULDER

EAT STRAINED BEETS

DON'T CRY

PLAY NICE

Dan Yaccarino

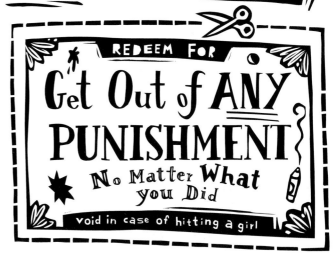

Robert Zimmerman

Biographies

Lisa Adams grew up in New England, graduated from Pratt Institute, and now lives and works in New York. Her illustrations, which are an unusual combination of pencil-rendered photo-realism and airbrushed cartoon elements, have appeared in the *New York Times Magazine, Child, American Baby,* and the *New Yorker.* Ms. Adams has designed a trademark teddy bear and line of corresponding products for BabyGap, for whom she also does illustration each season.

Maciek Albrecht is an illustrator who in 1990 founded Fabrika Studio, where he produces animated shorts, acting as both director and art director. In recent years, Mr. Albrecht has been dividing his time between New York and Poland when he is not traveling to other parts of the world.

Makiko Azakami is widely known in Japan for hand-cut 3-D paper sculptures called "Paper Toys," which have been exhibited in twenty-five solo shows in Japan and New York. In the United States, Ms. Azakami's paper toys have won Silver and Bronze Awards for Excellence at two "Dimensional Illustration" shows at the New York Art Director's Club and been exhibited at the American Crafts Museum. Commissions have followed from Random House, the *Atlantic Monthly,* MTV-VH1, and the Vera Wang Bridal Salon on Madison Avenue. Though best known for her paper toys, Ms. Azakami's pen and ink drawings are known to a small circle of collectors as pictorial/narrative diaries of her travels that she prints in limited editions. Ms. Azakami lives and works in Tokyo.

Charles Barsotti, originally from Texas, lives in Kansas City, where he draws cartoons for the *New Yorker* and many other publications. Mr. Barsotti spent several years with Hallmark, was cartoon editor for the *Saturday Evening Post,* did a daily spot for *USA Today* for eight years, and has been a contract artist with the *New Yorker* for over twenty years. Mr. Barsotti has done commercials for Japanese television and published five cartoon collections, including *A Girl Needs a Little Action, Kings Don't Carry Money,* and *Charles Barsotti's Texas.*

Michael Bartalos saw *Shadowville,* his first children's book, published in 1995. In addition to work done for clients like Sony Music, American Express, MTV, and Apple Computer, a sampling of Mr. Bartalos's most interesting projects include window display for Barneys New York and Bloomingdale's; the design of children's mannequins for Pucci International; and limited-edition letterpress books, posters, and post cards made in collaboration with Purgatory Pie Press. His books and prints are in various collections, including those of the Museum of Modern Art, the Cooper Hewitt Museum, the Metropolitan Museum, the New York Public Library Rare Book Collection, the Tate Gallery, and the Victoria and Albert Museum. Currently a resident of San Francisco, Mr. Bartalos travels extensively throughout Asia and spends much time in Japan, where he has almost as many illustration clients as he does in the United States.

Gary Baseman, not surprisingly, lists Groucho Marx, Elvis Costello, and Saul Steinberg among his influences. Mr. Baseman thrives on the deadline pressure of jobs for clients like *Time* magazine, Nike, Mercedes-Benz, AT&T, Apple Computer, and, most recently, Nickelodeon, for whom he created an animated TV show pilot.

Guy Billout was born in Decize, France, and worked as a designer in Paris ad agencies for a number of years before coming to New York to break into illustration. Since 1982, the *Atlantic Monthly* has given Mr. Billout a full page in every other issue to showcase his adroitly rendered visual puns. Recently, Mr. Billout was given a regular spot with complete freedom in *Le Monde,* the French newspaper. He has received numerous Gold and Silver awards from The Society of Illustrators and has written and illustrated six children's books, four of which were included in the *New York Times* list of the "Ten Best Children's Books" for the years they were released.

Maris Bishofs, originally from Latvia, lived in Russia, Israel, and France before coming to New York in 1982. Very much an international artist, Mr. Bishofs has won awards, exhibited his work, and received commissions for publications in Israel, Europe, South America, and the United States.

Mary Lynn Blasutta was born and raised in Columbus, Ohio, and studied at the Columbus College of Art and Design. A former art director and Manhattan resident, Ms. Blasutta now lives and illustrates in New Paltz, New York.

Cathie Bleck is the third in a family of nine children, seven of whom are professional artists. Ms. Bleck lives in Ohio with her husband and their three children and likes to travel someplace exotic at least once a year. She has found inspiration for her work in Japan, Singapore, Dominica, Israel, Scandinavia, Russia, Bali, Europe, and South Africa.

Barry Blitt, originally from Montreal, ranks the difficulty of his childhood somewhere between R. Crumb's and Brian Wilson's. Mr. Blitt currently resides in Greenwich, Connecticut, where he does his elegantly satirical ink drawings for the *New Yorker* as well as *Time, Rolling Stone,* the *Boston Globe, Entertainment Weekly,* and others.

Tom Bloom says he "grew up when pencils were still used for drawing," which may explain the pleasing familiarity of his pen and ink drawings. Mr. Bloom's genial illustrations can be found in the pages of *Fortune, Barron's,* the *New York Times,* and the *New Yorker,* among other publications.

Christopher S. Brown, an English artist, does somewhat primitive block prints filled with symbolic imagery. He teaches and lectures extensively in London and out, on fashion and textiles as well as general illustration and graphic design. In addition, Mr. Brown has written and illustrated articles on men's fashion for the London *Financial Times,* designed textiles, and curated exhibitions for FACTS, an AIDS information center in London.

Diana Bryan's paper cutout illustrations have appeared in countless magazines and newspapers and been made into two award-winning children's videos: *The Fisherman and His Wife,* narrated by Jodie Foster, and *The Monkey People,* narrated by the late Raul Julia. For the 1995 centennial anniversary of the New York Public Library, Ms. Bryan designed a continuous mural of images from what the library deemed the "Books of the Century." The installation lined the walls of the entire third-floor corridor of the Main Branch on Fifth Avenue and 42nd Street.

Dave Calver lives in a 1940s Tudor-style house filled with more than 500 pairs of salt and pepper shakers and 130 cookie jars. His sensuous colored-pencil illustrations have been commissioned for a wide range of projects and are particularly effective as book covers. In 1995, Running Book Press published Mr. Calver's miniature pop-up book titled *Crazy For You.*

Roz Chast is a *New Yorker* cartoonist with a devoted following. She has published seven volumes of her cartoons—*Last Resorts, Unscientific Americans, Parallel Universes, Poems and Songs, Mondo Boxo, The Four Elements,* and *Proof of Life on Earth*—and illustrated two children's books, *Now Everybody Really Hates Me* and *Gabby the Shrew.* Her third book for children, *Now I Will Never Leave the Dinner Table,* and a new cartoon collection devoted to the parent-child relationship are due out in 1996.

Seymour Chwast, a founding partner of the celebrated Pushpin Studios, is one of the most enduring and accomplished illustrators and graphic designers of our time. He has produced exceptional posters, animated films, advertising, corporate and environmental graphics, typefaces, books, magazines, music packaging, and theatrical backdrops. Mr. Chwast's distinctive work has been exhibited and honored in museums and galleries in Europe, Russia, Japan, Brazil, and the United States and is in the permanent collections of the Museum of Modern Art, the Smithsonian, the Library of Congress, the Cooper-Hewitt, and elsewhere.

Greg Clarke, a graduate of UCLA, lives and works in Santa Monica. A gifted graphic designer as well as an illustrator, Mr. Clarke's work has appeared in top national magazines and in ad campaigns for Fox TV, Intel Corporation, and Marriott Hotels. He exhibits his work with fellow artists Mark Fox and Gary Baseman under the collective name "WiseGeist."

Santiago Cohen, born in Mexico City, now calls Hoboken, New Jersey, home with his wife and their children. In addition to designing Christmas cards for the Museum of Modern Art, Mr. Cohen illustrates for a wide variety of magazines and newspapers and claims to be artistically influenced by his seven-year-old son and three-year-old daughter.

Paul Corio has illustrated for many publications but has done some of his most interesting work in small, semi-autobiographical books that were featured in "The Illustrated Book," a 1995 exhibition at the Center for Book Arts in New York. Also exhibited was Mr. Corio's comic book–style adaptation of Alfred Jarry's *Ubu Rex* from P.U. Publications. He has also played drums on five albums with various bands and was briefly apprenticed to a tattoo artist.

Isabelle Dervaux, a native of France who lived in New York for many years, recently moved to San Francisco with her husband and their small daughter. Ms. Dervaux's energetic and sparely drawn characters have often been used, to excellent effect, in packaging design. She has illustrated her first children's book and is now at work on drawings for a poetry collection.

Richard Downs, an alumnus of Art Center College of Design in California, has been a faculty member of its illustration department since 1989. His distinctively spiky drawing style has been featured in many important illustration annuals and journals and in publications as diverse as *Scholastic, RayGun, Ms.,* and the *Anchorage Daily News.*

Debbie Drechsler worked her way up as an illustrator through a local feminist paper, daily papers, and national magazines like *Spy, Esquire,* and *Ms.* before creating her own comic strips, which can be seen in *Drawn & Quarterly,* a comic periodical. Ms. Drechsler lives in northern California with two cats, two dogs and, conveniently, a veterinarian.

Regan Dunnick's B.F.A. is from the Ringling School of Art in Sarasota, where he presently teaches. Levi-Strauss, Pepsi, American Express, and Sony have commissioned illustrations from Mr. Dunnick, whose work has been recognized with many industry honors. His work is in the Library of Congress's permanent collections as well as in private collections in the United States and Japan.

Richard Egielski is best known for his award-winning illustration for children's books, including *Louis, The Fish; It Happened in Pinsk; Hey, Al;* and the *Tub People* series. Mr. Egielski studied at both Pratt Institute and Parsons School of Design and now lives in New Jersey with his wife, their son, and Daisy, the dog.

Carolyn Fisher, originally from western Canada, settled in Montana after living in New York for a number of years. In addition to her illustration, Ms. Fisher makes extraordinary, one-of-a-kind toys and books out of papier mâché and other media.

Jeffrey Fisher has lived and worked for extended periods in London; Melbourne, Australia (his hometown); and, at present, Paris. Other trips have taken him to Nepal, southeast Asia, and the United States. In addition to creating masterful book jacket design and editorial and corporate illustration, Mr. Fisher designed "Fisherfont," which won the fortieth annual Type Director's Club Award, and has had the honor of creating stamps illustrating the history of astronomy for the United Kingdom Royal Mail.

Douglas Fraser zoomed to the top of his profession almost before completing the School of Visual Arts' M.F.A. program in 1986. From the start, Mr. Fraser's exceptional talent has drawn commissions from blue-chip corporate, editorial, and publishing clients and earned him countless awards and honors. Especially notable are large-scale projects Mr. Fraser has undertaken, including a print, outdoor, and animation campaign for Lowenbrau; billboards for Levi Strauss; and five heroic murals in St. Louis's Powerhouse. After many years in New York, Mr. Fraser returned to Alberta, Canada, his place of birth, to live, work, and teach.

Gale was born in England and raised there, as well as in Malaysia and Malta. As an adult, he has lived and traveled throughout Africa, Scotland, Germany, and the United States. His versatile career has included painting; animated filmmaking; editorial and book illustration; extensive travel journals; theatrical stage sets; the production of "Weltschmertz," an experimental opera (in which he also performed); landscape studies along the Berlin Wall, commissioned by the West Berlin Senate; and a mural at Schoenberg Art Center, also in Berlin.

Janie Geiser is an internationally recognized creator/director of avant-garde puppet theater as well as an illustrator. The 1992 recipient of a Guggenheim Fellowship, Ms. Geiser's Obie Award–winning theater work has been funded by the NEA (in both the Visual Arts and Theater categories), the New York State Council on the Arts, and the Henson Foundation. Ms. Geiser also makes one-of-a-kind and limited-edition books, one of which is in the Artist's Book Collection at the Museum of Modern Art.

David Goldin has traveled extensively throughout the Far East, India, Greece, and Europe collecting fascinating ephemera to incorporate into personal collages and illustrations. Mr. Goldin's jam-packed journals were featured in the 1995 "Illustrated Book" show at the Center for Book Arts in New York, and *Lost Cat,* his first book for children, is due out in the spring of 1996.

Julia Gorton uses an atypical airbrush technique to create her unique and fresh illustrations. Especially appealing are *The Gumdrop Tree, Riddle Rhymes,* and *My New Sandbox,* three children's books she has both designed and illustrated. Ms. Gorton lives outside of New York with her husband (also an illustrator) and their three children and teaches at the Parsons School of Design.

Josh Gosfield has been a carpenter, a door-to-door salesman, and, for a number of years, the art director of *New York* magazine. His oil and acrylic paintings, often incorporating quirky trademark lettering and found materials, are commissioned by clients like the *New Yorker, Manner Vogue* (Germany), *Rolling Stone* and the *New York Times.*

Rodney Alan Greenblat's talents extend beyond illustration to include sculpture, drawing, painting, computer graphics, and animation. Mr. Greenblat's passion for the computer has yielded three software programs for children: *Rodney's Funscreen, Rodney's Wonder Window,* and *Dazzeloids.* Mr. Greenblat has also written and illustrated three children's books titled *Uncle Wizmo's New Used Car, Aunt Ippy's Museum of Junk,* and *Slombo the Gross.* Commissioned in 1992 by the Chrysler Museum in Norfolk, Virginia, Mr. Greenblat created a touring narrative show called "Land-Ho: The Mythic World of Rodney Alan Greenblat," a walk-through storybook of eighty-five paintings, wooden sculptures, mechanical objects, and computer graphics. "Rodney Guy," an animated segment of a weekly children's show called *Ugo Ugo Lhuga,* can currently be seen on Japanese TV.

Gene Greif, formerly an art director, has been creating distinctive collage illustrations for national magazines and Fortune 500 companies since 1984. In 1995 Mr. Greif co-founded Bent Studio, extending his scope to children's books, animation, and

murals. Examples of Mr. Greif's work are in the permanent collections of the Museum of Modern Art, the Smithsonian Institute, and the Pompidou Center in Paris.

Steven Guarnaccia, a prolific illustrator, designer, writer, and lecturer, fills a unique niche in the field of illustration. Interested in moving more towards product design, Mr. Guarnaccia has created collections of silver jewelry, neckties, clocks, greeting cards, toys, wall-mounted iron "signs," and limited-edition rugs. He has authored *A Stiff Drink and a Close Shave,* a compendium of men's accessories and activities from the stylish years of the 1930s to the 1950s, with Bob Sloan; *Designing for Children* with Steven Heller; and *Skeleton Closet,* a book for children published in 1996. Mr. Guarnaccia's work was included in "New Pop," a grand-scale overview of contemporary illustration that opened at the Museo Fortuny in Venice and traveled to Milan, where his work was also featured in two 1995 solo shows.

Eric Hanson, a Minneapolis-based artist, is probably best known for charming maps and pen and ink and watercolor drawings. An avid skier, Mr. Hanson has been an editor and traveling correspondent for *Skiing* magazine for many years and is currently working on a book about skiing in different parts of the world. Several of Mr. Hanson's maps are part of the British Museum's permanent collection.

Jessie Hartland lives and works in a loft in New York City's financial district with her husband and their son. Ms. Hartland's work has appeared in many publications in the United States and Japan, where her work is also well known. Current projects include writing and illustrating her first children's book and promotional booklets for Gilbert Paper as well as designing watches for Swatch. Ms. Hartland adds these endeavors to a resume that includes window installations for Barneys New York, a mural for Esprit, the animated movie trailer for Spaulding Gray's *Monster In A Box,* and a cat's-head-shaped book, *Cat Cut,* published in 1992.

Pamela Hobbs, an English illustrator, is one of the new-wave artists designing and illustrating by computer. Having recently left New York and the faculties of the School of Visual Arts and the New School for Social Research, Ms. Hobbs is now teaching computer graphics at the California College of Arts and Crafts. Ms. Hobbs's work has been written about and exhibited extensively in the United States and Japan.

David Johnson, known for elegant and incisive pen and ink portraits in the *New York Times* and other places says, "About my life heretofore, the less that is said, the better it is understood."

William Joyce is the illustrator and author of *George Shrinks, Dinosaur Bob and His Adventures with the Family Lazardo, Nicholas Cricket, A Day with Wilbur Robinson, Bently & egg,* and *Santa Calls,* all children's books that became instant prize-winning classics. Mr. Joyce's lifelong love of movies may be fulfilled when his stories leap from page to screen. In the works are *A Day with Wilbur Robinson* (with Disney/Touchstone) and *Santa Calls* (with American Zoetrope). Mr. Joyce created paintings as "pre-production inspiration" for Disney's first fully computer-animated feature film, *Toy Story,* and Fox TV is developing animated versions of *George Shrinks* and *Bently & egg* as Saturday morning children's programs. Mr. Joyce lives in Shreveport, Louisiana, with his wife and their two children.

Maira Kalman is the author and illustrator of *Hey Willy, See the Pyramids; Sayonara, Mrs. Kackleman; Max Makes a Million; Ooh-la-la, Max in Love; Max in Hollywood, Baby; Chicken Soup, Boots;* and *Swami on Rye, Max in India.* She recently returned, with her husband and their two children, to New York after a year in Rome where she consumed fresh figs and practiced her Italian.

Victoria Kann executes her elegant collages in a small studio surrounded by stacks of old *Popular Mechanics,* obsolete encyclopedias, and obscure medical textbooks. Her work has been featured on the covers of *Newsweek, Harper's,* and *Business Week.* A graduate of the Rhode Island School of Design, Ms. Kann lives in New York and teaches collage illustration at the School of Visual Arts.

Bruce Eric Kaplan lives in Los Angeles and draws cartoons that appear in the *New Yorker.*

Sean Kelly studied at the Rhode Island School of Design and graduated from neighboring Brown University. Before settling in New York City, Mr. Kelly worked on staff at the *Miami Herald* and moved to Washington, D.C., where he began freelancing as an illustrator. His drawings often appear in the *New York Times* as well as the *Washington Post,* the *Boston Globe,* and *George* magazine.

J. D. King claims to have "wasted" the years from 1977 to 1985 as a member of a "progressive garage-rock" band, an underground comic artist and, for a brief time, as an advertising copywriter. Since getting serious about illustration in the mideighties, Mr. King's graphic, geometric work has been in *The Art of Mickey Mouse, The Art of Barbie, Drawn & Quarterly,* the *New Yorker,* an Absolut Vodka ad, on many jazz CD covers, and in numerous other magazines and publications.

Daniel Kirk illustrates in oils for many advertising and editorial clients, but is happiest creating picture books for children. He is the writer and illustrator of *Skateboard Monsters, Lucky's 24-Hour Garage,* and *Trash Trucks!* and has illustrated several books by other writers as well.

Michael Klein may be the only illustrator working today who graduated magna cum laude with a B.S. in economics from Wharton Business School. After three years as an ad agency media planner, Mr. Klein studied illustration at Parsons School of Design and has been illustrating full-time ever since. With the help of his two small daughters, Mr. Klein has become proficient on the Magna-Doodle.

Robert Kopecky was born in San Diego and attended Art Center College of Design in Pasadena. He has worked in animation, publication, and poster design and as a drawing and illustration teacher at Otis-Parsons in Los Angeles and the Academy of Art in San Francisco. Mr. Kopecky divides his time between New York and Arizona, working as an illustrator, designer, and comic artist.

Anita Kunz lives in Toronto, where she produces the critically acclaimed gouache and watercolor paintings that have been featured in *Graphis* (Switzerland), *Communication Arts, Idea Magazine* (Japan), and *Applied Arts* (Canada) and used in campaigns by countless international magazines, book publishers, and advertising agencies. Ms. Kunz frequently lectures at universities and institutions, including the Smithsonian in Washington, D.C., and has exhibited her work in galleries worldwide.

Peter Kuper was named "Hot Cartoonist" of 1995 by *Rolling Stone* magazine due in part to "Eye of the Beholder," his nationally syndicated strip, which first ran in the *New York Times; GIVE IT UP!,* a comic-strip adaptation of Franz Kafka's shorter works, and *Stripped,* an unauthorized autobiography. An avid traveler, Mr. Kuper published *ComicsTrips,* an account of eight months in Africa and southeast Asia. In addition, Mr. Kuper is co-editor of the political comic/magazine *World War 3;* an art director of *INX,* a syndicated political illustration group; and an instructor of a course in "Alternative Comics" at the School of Visual Arts.

Philippe Lardy, a native of Switzerland, moved to New York City in 1987 to attend the School of Visual Arts. Mr. Lardy's illustration clients include the *New York Times, Newsweek, Esquire, Rolling Stone,* Bloomingdale's, and AT&T. Mr. Lardy, his wife, and their two children divide each year between New York and Geneva, Switzerland.

Tim Lewis, a native of Michigan, was an illustrator and designer at Push Pin Studios in the early years and presently lives in Brooklyn, where he produces innovative illustration, including a recent contribution to *The Art of Barbie.*

Ross MacDonald was born and raised in what he describes as numerous remote corners of Canada. He left school to apprentice as a printer and typesetter but has no other formal art training. He now lives and works in New York City, where some of his more interesting projects have included graphics for *Saturday Night Live* commercial parodies, title design for two John Hughes films, illustrations for children's books, and a stamp for the Canadian Postal Service. Mr. MacDonald's award-winning, retro graphic style has been honored by many industry publications and organizations. He has been on the faculty of the Banff Publishing Workshop since the mid-1980s.

Stan Mack's *Real Life American Revolution,* a history of the Revolutionary era done in his trademark narrative comic-strip style, was published 1995 and awarded ALA's "Best Book for Young Adults," YALSA's "Best Book for Reluctant Readers," and named the New York Public Library's 1995 "Book for the Teen Age." In the same year, Mr. Mack collaborated with Janet Bode on *Heartbreak and Roses,* a story collection of real-life teenage relationships. These projects are natural outgrowths of Mr. Mack's long-running "Real-Life Funnies" in the *Village Voice* and "Out-Takes" in *Adweek* magazine.

Michael Maslin has been a *New Yorker* cartoonist since 1977 and has published four collections of his work, titled *The More the Merrier, The Gang's All Here, The Crowd Goes Wild,* and *Mixed Company.* Recent projects include *Fathers & Sons,* a cartoon collection co-edited with Liza Donnelly, his wife, herself a cartoonist and children's book author, and *Husbands & Wives,* a joint collection of their cartoons.

Bill Mayer's award-winning, versatile airbrush illustration is in great demand by clients like U.S. Steel, Georgia Pacific, Anheuser-Busch, *Playboy,* the *Wall Street Journal,* and *Business Week.* Mr. Mayer notes as a most satisfying project the illustrations he did for a Showtime children's video production of *Br'er Rabbit and Boss Lion,* narrated by Danny Glover and scored by Dr. John. Mr. Mayer lives with his wife, also an artist, in Decatur, Georgia.

Patrick McDonnell does a daily and Sunday comic strip called "Mutts" for King Features Syndicate that stars Earl, his real-life Jack Russell terrier. Mr. McDonnell also draws "Bad Baby," a monthly strip for *Parents* magazine that Hallmark is developing as an animated feature-length movie for television. Mr. McDonnell recently animated a television commercial for the New York Philharmonic in addition to pursuing illustration projects for corporate and editorial clients.

Paul Meisel has, in addition to advertising and editorial work, illustrated numerous children's books, including *Busy Buzzing Bumblebees, My World & Globe, I Am Really a Princess,* and *Your Insides.* He lives in Connecticut with his wife and their three sons.

Paula Munck, born in Australia, is in demand by a stellar list of corporate and editorial clients seeking her fluid, vibrant gouache paintings. Some notable commissions include large-scale murals, a Shiseido Cosmetics contract for eight *Beauty Book* covers and, for Nynex, the covers of 250 regional phone books for 1993–94. After several years of living in Toronto and spending the cold months in Jamaica, Ms. Munck has settled in Miami, where she is surrounded by the light and color that inspire her award-winning work.

Gregory Nemec feels that the technique he has chosen has much to do with his strictly Catholic upbringing and the Midwestern work ethic tempered by *Mad* magazine. Citing Italo Calvino, Rockwell Kent, and Tim Burton as influences on his work, which he aptly describes as "meticulous and labor-intensive," Mr. Nemec has come to live and work in New York via South Dakota and Iowa, where he was born and raised, and Philadelphia's University of the Arts, where he received his degree in art.

Robert Neubecker is the illustrator that art directors call when the issue is thorny and the desired solution is penetrating but not heavy-handed. Mr. Neubecker has illustrated award-winning covers for *Newsweek, Global Finance,* and *Time International,* in addition to projects for a broad range of editorial and corporate clients. After many years in New York, Mr. Neubecker now lives in Utah, has recently married, teaches illustration at Brigham Young University, and skis as much as possible.

Christian Northeast's work has appeared on compact disc covers, in magazines like *Rolling Stone* and *Ray Gun,* and on the cover of *American Illustration 13.* Mr. Northeast lives in Toronto and will rake lawns and shovel snow for extra cash.

John O'Brien has illustrated more than thirty books and numerous *Highlights* magazine covers for children, in addition to his well-known *New Yorker* cartoons. Mr. O'Brien spends winters in Miami and summers in Wildwood, New Jersey,

where he works by day as a lifeguard and moonlights at night as a riverboat banjo player.

Gary Panter is a cartoonist/illustrator/painter who won three Emmys as Production Designer for *Pee-Wee's Playhouse,* was head designer for Pee Wee Toys, and designed the Children's Playroom at the ultra-hip Paramount Hotel in New York. His work has appeared in underground and mainstream publications including *Raw, Interview, Spin,* and *Time* and as cover art on numerous compact discs.

Evan Polenghi was born in New York City and raised in Italy. Mr. Polenghi conveys the exuberant influence of that culture in the deeply detailed illustration he creates in his New York studio.

Kee Rash lives in Phoenix, Arizona, and worked as a newspaper and freelance artist for a number of years before pursuing illustration as a career. His work appeared in *American Illustration 13* and has been commissioned by a growing list of newspapers and national magazines.

Victoria Roberts grew up in Mexico and Australia and now lives in New York. Ms. Roberts's drawings have appeared in many publications including the *New Yorker, Playboy, Ms.,* and the *New York Times. Cattitudes,* a full-color tribute to felines, is the most recent addition to nearly twenty books she has illustrated. Ms. Roberts enjoys endangered domestic pastimes like petit-point, rug hooking, and china painting.

Lilla Rogers's illustrations, usually incorporating her trademark hand-lettering, have been commissioned by over one hundred magazines and countless corporate and publishing clients in the United States and abroad. Ms. Rogers's work has been exhibited in Paris, Venice, New York, and Tokyo, where she has had two solo shows and is currently visible in a national print campaign for Levi Strauss. Ms. Rogers works and teaches in the Boston area.

Marc Rosenthal studied architecture at Princeton and was a designer with Milton Glaser for five years before making a career in illustration and painting. Mr. Rosenthal recently completed a traveling exhibition of geography for kids, commissioned by the Smithsonian Institute. He lives in upstate New York with his wife and their son.

Anthony Russo is well known for two styles of illustration, both with a primitive spirit: black and white work in scratchboard and color work in acrylic, watercolor, and oil crayon. Mr. Russo's award-winning illustration is used for a wide variety of corporate and editorial projects and is favored especially for brilliant book jacket design. Mr. Russo lived for a time in Tuscany and has traveled in Thailand, Nepal, England, Germany, Austria, Jamaica, Peru, Iceland, and, most recently, Belize and Costa Rica. He lives in Rhode Island with his wife and their son.

Richard Sala's comics were first published in *Raw Magazine* and have since been collected in four books, titled *Hypnotic Tales, Thirteen O'Clock, Black Cat Crossing,* and *The Ghastly Ones.* In addition to illustrating for magazines like *Esquire, Newsweek,* and *Playboy,* Mr. Sala has created "Invisible Hands," an animated serial for MTV, and contributed to *The Resident's Freak Show* CD-ROM.

Isabel Samaras, San Francisco–based "bad girl," paints pop-culture-inspired erotica on trays, lunch boxes, and ceramics. Ms. Samaras's work has been featured in many west coast exhibitions, including the recent "See No Evil," an exploration of censorship that was itself censored, with curtains covering Ms. Samaras's work and that of others. Ms. Samaras continues to pursue her artistic obsession with dead presidents, TV sit-coms, Japanese monsters, rock personalities, and comic book anti-heroes.

J. Otto Seibold, the illustrator and co-author of *Mr. Lunch Takes a Plane Ride, Mr. Lunch Borrows a Canoe,* and *Monkey Business* is also an award-winning animation designer. Prior to his illustration career, Mr. Seibold worked at the Clorox Bleach Research Center, where he designed nose-sized doors for a kitty litter testing booth and a public fountain in the form of a monumental Clorox bottle.

Danny Shanahan, a regular *New Yorker* contributor, has published a collection of his cartoons titled *Lassie! Get Help!* and, most recently, *Buckledown, the Workhound,* his first children's book.

Maddalena Sisto, an architect, writes and illustrates articles about young international artists, design trends, and fashion for Rizzoli, Mondadori, and Condé Nast publications. Ms. Sisto's own work as a designer and artist has included towering couture-clad women for Milan's prêt-à-porter fashion shows and a collection of ceramic teapots in the shape of women's heads, each with four interchangeable hat-shaped lids. Ms. Sisto's work has been exhibited in Stockholm, Tokyo, New York, and many Italian cities including Milan, where she lives.

Michael Sloan, after graduating from the Rhode Island School of Design, spent several years traveling and living in the Middle East, Holland, and Italy before working as a printmaker in Paris. Mr. Sloan currently lives in Brooklyn, illustrates for a wide range of clients, collects stamps, and plays in his rock band, WOOZY.

Elwood H. Smith was an art director in Chicago before establishing himself as an illustrator and moving to New York City. Mr. Smith's illustrations have appeared in countless publications and in ad campaigns for clients like Sony, AT&T, Nabisco, Carlsburg Beer, and Cellular One. In addition, he has written and illustrated two books for children and collaborated on animation projects at the Ink Tank in New York. Artists who have inspired Mr. Smith's work are Rube Goldberg, George Herriman (Krazy Kat), and Billy DeBeck (Barney Google). Mr. Smith and his wife live and work in Rhinebeck, New York.

Nancy Speir lives in Sonoma County in northern California with her husband, their two dogs, five cats, and an Arabian gelding that Ms. Speir is training in Endurance Trail Riding. She tones down her wild and crazy personal work for magazines, kid's books, and greeting cards and is currently illustrating the first children's book she herself has written.

Art Spiegelman is a co-founder and editor of *Raw,* the acclaimed magazine of avant-garde comics and graphics. Probably best known for *Maus: A Survivor's Tale,* a two-volume autobiographical account of growing up as the child of Auschwitz survivors, Mr. Spiegelman is responsible for a powerful work of graphic and narrative art. Original drawings and working studies from *Maus* were exhibited at the Museum of Modern Art in 1991 and Mr. Spiegelman was awarded a Pulitzer prize for the opus in 1992. More recently, Mr. Spiegelman illustrated Joseph Moncure March's lost classic, *The Wild Party,* and has become a contributing artist to the *New Yorker.* Mr. Spiegelman lives in New York with his wife and their two children.

Joost Swarte lives in the Netherlands and has had a brilliant and varied career as an artist, designer, and animator. His crisp and funny ink drawings, reminiscent of John Held, Jr., and Gluyas Williams, have been turned into music packaging, posters, postage stamps, MTV commercials, and theatrical backdrops and books. Mr. Swarte's work has been widely exhibited in the Netherlands, throughout Europe, and in the United States.

Dan Yaccarino's work has appeared in countless magazines and publications in the United States and abroad. He is the author and illustrator of *Big Brother Mike,* an award-winning children's book and true-to-life tale of sibling-tormented childhood. In his spare time, Mr. Yaccarino creates wonderful one-of-a-kind, often mechanical, toys and objects.

Robert Zimmerman has, after a stretch in New York, returned to the mountains of North Carolina with his wife and their two children. Commissioned by a wide range of editorial and corporate clients, "Zimm" produces more and more of his graphic, antic illustrations on the amazing computer.

Pam Sommers opened the Illustration Gallery in New York in 1988 as a showcase of contemporary original illustration. Ms. Sommers closed the Gallery in 1994 and now shows and sells art privately from the Manhattan loft she shares with her husband Peter Ellers and Henry, their smooth fox terrier.